LONDON'S LIBERTIES

OR
A Learned Argument of Law and Reason

Published by *The Rota* at the University of Exeter
1972

© The Rota, 1972

ISBN : 0 9501950 2 2

Printed and Bound by Short Run Press Ltd., Exeter, Devon

Bibliographical Note

London's liberties is a report of a debate on London's constitution. On the one side are the spokesmen for the reformers who propose that the Lord Mayor and sheriffs be elected indirectly by representatives of the wards; on the other are the counsel for the Livery Companies defending the existing method of election by Common Hall. Published by Giles Calvert, well-known as publisher of many Leveller and Digger tracts, the pamphlet probably formed part of the reformers' campaign. Thomason dated his copy December 19, just five days after the debate. The politics of this period are treated by James E. Farnell, 'The usurpation of honest London householders: Barebone's Parliament', *English Historical Review*, 82 (1967), esp. pp. 33-43. Dr Valerie Pearl, who has kindly helped with this note, will treat London politics during the Puritan revolution in a forthcoming book.

The arguments, like those in the Putney debates, combine the examination of historical and legal precedent (often narrowly antiquarian) with exposition of the general principles of rightful government. John Wildman does most of the speaking for the insurgents. Although he withdrew from Leveller politics in 1649, he deploys Leveller rhetoric to establish a method of election favourable to the Godly party. With him is the pamphleteering Independent, John Price, who was a member of Goodwin's congregation at Coleman street and the putative author of *Walwins wiles*.

How seriously this attack was taken is indicated by the appearance for the Livery Companies of three of the most eminent lawyers of the period: John Maynard, Matthew Hale (here Hales) and John Wilde (or Wylde). All had been prominent in the Long Parliament; all took the Engagement; all survived the Restoration; all held high judicial office at various times. (For them, see the *D.N.B.*)

The tract was reprinted in 1682 to oppose Charles II's attack on the City's charter. The title page announces not merely the debate on the franchise and the examination of ancient charters, but also that the participants agreed that these charters confirm former rights. A new preface piously hopes that the opinions of the three great oracles of the law will decide the differences between the citizens that adhere to the Lord Mayor and those (the Whigs) that adhere to the sheriffs. (This preface replaces 'The Publisher to the Reader'.)

London's liberties is reprinted from the copy in the Thomason Collection which is identical with others in the British Museum and in the Bodleian. It is reproduced with the permission of the Trustees of the British Museum. Shelf mark: E. 620. (7). Wing, *Short title catalogue*, L2936A.

London's Liberties;

OR A
LEARNED ARGVMENT
OF
LAVV & REASON,
UPON
Saturday, December 14. 1650.

Before the Lord Major, Court of Aldermen, and Common-Councell at Guild Hall, LONDON,

Between { Mr Maynard, Mr Hales & Mr Wilde } Of Councell for the Companies of London.

And { Major John Wildman and Mr John Price } Of Councell for the Freemen of London.

Wherein the Freedom of the Citizens of LONDON in their Elections of their chief Officers, is fully Debated, the most Ancient Charters and Records of the City examined, and the principles of just Government cleared & vindicated.

This Discourse was exactly taken in Short-hand by severall that were present at the Argument, who have compared their Notes, and published them for Publique use.

London, Printed by Ja. Cottrel for Gyles Calvert at the sign of the black spread Eagle at the West-end of Pauls, 1651. 1650.

The Publisher to the Reader.

GENTLEMEN,

WHen the House is not mine, you cannot expect that I should build the Porch: Yet 'tis but reasonable, that having offered the House to your view, I should shew you the Way that Leads unto it; I mean, the Occasion of the following Discourse. Please then to be informed, that some Good men of the Common-Councell perceiving the Cities Poverty (the CHAMBER of London being utterly exhausted, and the poor Orphans Portions expended) moved the Court that a Committee might be Chosen to examine the Accounts of the CHAMBER; which was Ordered: And the Committee having Examined, made this following Report.

August 26. 1650.

The Report of the Committee appointed for Examination of the state of the CHAMBER of London.

About 1630. we finde the Chamber to be indebted about the sum of } 050000.00.00.

At Michaelmasse 1649. the Accompt of the Chamber being then Cast up, the Chamber was then in Debt: Viz.   l.   s.   d.

To Orphans   169654:01:03½ } 264066.14.05¼
To other Persons for Principall money 094412:13:04

The means whereby it came into Debt, are either Extraordinary, or Ordinary.

Extraordinary.

		l. s. d.
	A Gold Cup given the Prince	001191.04.05
Anno 1633.	Presents given to the King, Queen, and Prince	003260.00.00
Anno 1634	A Jewell given the Queen	004000.00.00
Anno 1634	Entertainment of the King and Queen at Merchant-Taylors-Hall.	001287.12.08
Anno 1634	Christening the Duke of York	000633.00.00
Anno 1639	A Cup of gold given the Q. Mother, & other charges	001000.00.00
Anno 1639	Charges of the Charter	002355.00.00
Anno 1639	Given the King	010000.00.00
Anno 1635	Composition for Package and Scavage	004000.00.00
Anno 1639	Composition for London-Derry	012000.00.00
Anno 1639	To the repair of Pauls	000600.00.00
Anno 1642	Entertainment of the King and Queen	001786.00.00
	For Building the Bridge	006400.00.00
	For Ship-money, and setting out Ships at Sea	017218.00.00
	By Gifts and Rewards to Officers for 20 years, at 1200 l. per Annum }	024000.00.00
		089730.17.01
☞ Quære, What authority the Court of Aldermen had to give such gifts		
	By severall bad Debts	071739.14.01

Ordinary.

	l. s. d.
Charges for Marshall Causes for twenty years	035278.00.00
For Interest-money paid 20 years, at 6000 l. per annum	120000.00.00
By delivering up of Bonds to be Cancelled by Act of Common-Councell in 1640. to severall Persons for money lent them out of the Chamber 20. years before about 30000. l. Principall in all with Interest }	060000.00.00

For Officers standing Fees for about 20. years, at 1400 *l. per annum*   028000.00.00.
For Workmens wages for 20. years at 1000 *l. per annum*   020000.00.00
Stuff for Reparation for about 20. years, at 1600 *l. per annum*   030400.00.00

The totall sum given, lost and expended for about 20 years, is   455148.11.02

Present,

August 16. 1650.

Mr. Sheriff *Pack*
Mr. Ald. *Chiverton*
Col. *Mannering*
Mr. *Cole.*
Mr. *Barbone*
Mr. *Dallison*

Mr. Ald. *Titchborne*
Mr Ald. *Hayes*
Mr. *Gibbs*
Mr. *Bolton*
Mr. *Adams*
Mr. *Manton.*

Those good Men being very sensible of this horrid abuse of the City, that the CHAMBER, *which hath been esteemed like that among the* Romans, *a Sacred Treasury, for safety and pitying the Orphans crys. And searching how the City came to be thus* Bankrupt; *It was found that the chief Officers had been very faulty; and thereupon it was considered how they were Elected; and there arose the Question about the right of Electing the chief Officers of the City. And it came into debate whether the* Livery-men *ought to be the Electors, as now they are. Thereupon the Companies of* London *Petitioned the Court that they might continue their Elective power: And divers Freemen of the City petitioned for the abolishing that power of the Liveries or Companies: the Petitions are these.*

TO

To the right Honourable the Lord Major of the Citie of LONDON; and to the right Worshipfull the Aldermen his Brethren, and the Commons in Common Councell assembled.

The humble Petition of the severall Companies and Societies of the Citie of LONDON.

Humbly sheweth,

THat whereas it appeareth, That heretofore for divers yeares, many great differences did arise within this Citie, touching the election of the Lord Major and Sheriffes, to the great disturbance of the peace thereof; the said Elections being made divers and severall wayes, and with continuall alterations and often disturbances, *viz.* in the seventh yeare of King *Edward* the third, by the Major and Aldermen together, with the most sufficient men of every Ward, in the eighth yeare of the said King, as the Kings Proclamation then commanded; By the Aldermen, and the most discreet and ablest Citizens of the City; In the twentyeth year of that King, by the Major and all the Aldermen, and 12, 8, or 6, of every Ward, according as the Ward should be great or smal, of the richest and wisest men of every Ward: In the fiftieth year of the said King, by a certain number of the good men of the severall Mysteries (their Names being certified by the severall Companies.) In the eighth year of King *Richard* the second, by the Common-councell, and the most sufficient men of the City. In the ninth yeare of that King, by those as should be summoned of the most sufficient men of the Citie, or of the Common Councell. In the seventh yeare of King *Edward* the fourth, by the Generall Councell, the Masters and Wardens of every Mystery

of

of the Citie comming in their Liveries; and by other good men, especially summoned, and so the said unsetled Elections continued with many disturbances) untill in the 15. yeare of the said King *Edward* the fourth. That the same Election was setled by authoritie of this honorable Court of General Councell, by an Act then made, That the Master and Wardens of the Mysteries of this Citie, meeting in their Halls, or other fit places, and associating with the good men of the Company, clothed in their last Liveries, should come together to the *Guild-Hall* of this Citie for the election of the Major and Sheriffe. And that no other but the good men of the Common Councell of the Citie should be present at the said Elections; which courſe and custome hath been ever since yearly used and continued, to the honour, peace and happinesse of this Citie, and the well setled government of the same.

That the said Companies in obedience to Parliament, and for the honour, service, and safety of the Common-wealth and Citie, and in their good affections to both, have from time to time hazarded their persons, exhausted their meanes, and freely undergone all services, taxations, and charges imposed on them. And that so great a part of the government of this City is now setled in the severall Companies, that if a disturbance thereof be made, it may be feared in time to bring a ruine upon the whole.

And forasmuch as the Petitioners are given to understand, that there is an endevouring to deprive, and take from them, that their ancient & lawful right, for the election of Lor. Major & Sheriffes, which for neer two hundred yeares together, they and their predecessors (the Livery men of the severall Companies) have lawfully and quietly enjoyed, as belonging to them, without any question or disturbance.

Their humble desire and request therefore is, That this Honourable Court will be pleased to take their just cauſe into your serious consideration, that as they are for the most part the ancientest and most able Citizens of this Citie, and doe undergoe (as alwayes they have done) the greatest part of the charge, and service within the ſame; ſo

they

they may not be put from that their right of election, as they and their predecessors, Livery men, have (without alteration or disturbance, lovingly and peaceably) held and enjoyed ever since the said Act of the 15. *of* Edward *the fourth, being neere two hundred yeares, as aforesaid, or be discouraged from bearing charge, giving attendance, and performing services, as they have alwayes done, and performed for the honour and good of this Citie. And they shall, according to their duties, pray, &c.*

Tho. Chamberlain
William Barbe. } Mercers.

John Garrard,
John Southwood. } Skinners.

Samuel Harfnet,
William Hulme. } Grocers.

Geo. Alpers
Rich. Orme. } Merchant-Taylors.

Francis Pecke,
Peter Jones. } Drapers.

John Green, Haberdasher.
John Redding, Salter.
Rob. Gravenor, Ironmonger.

Tho. Lusher.
Gyles Baggs. } Fishmongers.

Wil. Feild.
Wil. James. } Vintners.

John Terry.
John Perrin. } Goldsmiths.

John Milles,
Edward Chard } Cloth-workers.

J. Sadler.

To the right Honorable, the Lord Major, Aldermen, and Commons in Common Councel Assembled.

The humble Petition of divers Freemen; Inhabitants of this honorable City;

Shewth,

THat whereas the Ancient Liberties of the City did admit only Freemen of the same, to have his Vote in the choice of the Supreme Magistrates thereof: The imposition of Governours upon a People without their voluntary Election, importing the prevalency of meer Tyranny and slavery ; And whereas the Livery-men of each Company thereof not chosen either by the City, or their respective Companies, and therefore not Representees, either of the one or the other, have for many years past, imposed such Supreme Magistrates upon the same City as they pleased, without the suffrage of the Freemen thereof, either by themselves or Representees chosen for that purpose. And lastly, whereas it hath pleased the Parliament of England to impose several Protestations, Vowes, and Covenants, upon your Petitioners, to preserve the Just and Native Liberties of the Subject, the price of much Blood and Treasure spent in this Nation, to recover and preserve the same; and for which end, your Petitioners humbly conceive this Court hath been Constituted, and sworn upon the election of the Representative Members thereof in their several Wards:

The premises considered, the Petitioners humbly pray, that by an Act of this honorable Court, such a competent number of Representees may be annually chosen by the Freemen of every Ward, in their respective Wards, who together with the Common Councel-men, may be authorized to choose the Supreme Officers of this City annually for the time to come. And your Petitioners shall pray, &c.

THese were referred to a Committee, & Counsel for the Companies there heard, And Mr. *Price* in the behalf of the Freemen : from thence it was referred to be fully debated before the Lord Major, Court of Aldermen and Common Councel. And on Saturday the 14. of *December*, the Court being sat at *Guild Hall*, the Companies brought for their Counsel, Mr. *Maynard*, Mr. *Hales*, and Mr. *Wilde*, Gentlemen most famous in the profession of the Law ; and the Freemen (besides Mr. *John Price*) had prevailed by much intreaty, with Major *John Wildman*, as I am informed, without hopes of Fees or rewards to plead their Cause ; and so the debate begun as followeth.

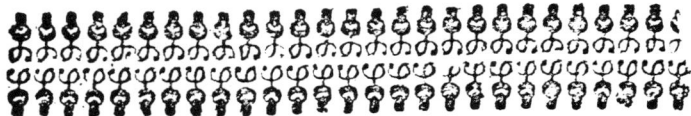

Mr. Price.

My Lord,

Only crave leave to speak one word in the behalf of my self; for I acknowledge my self to be but weak in the knowledge of the Law; and I therefore unable to withstand those Gentlemen of the long robe, come only as a Citizen of *London*, to render a reason of my subscribing of that Petition that was presented unto your Honor and this worshipful Court; And I hope you will not judge otherwise of my appearing here at this time. We began the last time to speak of it, to vindicate it to them that opposed us herein; And they being the first that spake then, we desire that they may likewise begin now, and then with your Lordships favor, we shall reply to them; for my part, I thought there had been an issue put to the businefs, and little thought had I to appear any more about it.

Mr. Recorder.

They that oppose any thing that is setled, to the end to have it altered, they usually begin first to shew their grounds or Reasons in all Courts of Justice.

Mr. Mainard.

The intent of our coming here, is not to introduce any novelty, but to maintain the ancient priviledges of this Famous City, under which it hath for so many hundreds of yeers flourished, in all Happinefs the earth affords, with Peace and Plenty.

And therefore we conceive we shall not need to produce any arguments to defend our cause, but to answer the objections that shall be made by such that do oppose us in the injoying our right, always presuming that where the poffeffion goeth, there the right is; and therefore if they on the other side have any thing to object, we are ready to give answers to their objections.

Mr. *Price*.

We hope we are before such men as will not take notice so much of the persons as of the arguments that are brought on both sides; And therefore my Lord, I shall begin to proceed where they please. The last time this business was under consideration before the worshipful Committee to be heard, the business was driven, as I conceive, to this head by our Opponents, to know whether the thing desired by us, be in your power to grant to us; And whether the things desired by them, were in your power to deny them.

They pleaded by their Councel, that they maintained their priviledges by right of custome, so that it was argued that the Law of Election was not in this Courts power to give.

So that your Lordship and this Honorable Court are by them made not so much as Judges, much less Parties.

Mr. Recorder.

Mr. *Price* takes it for granted, that all this Court understands the State of this Case, which they do not; and therefore I desire the question may be rightly stated that is to be disputed upon, otherwise you will spend much time and run into confusion, and it will be impossible for them that hear you to understand the business; so that I desire the Question may be stated and the matter of Fact agreed upon.

Mr. *Price*.

My Lord, I had thought to begin where we left the last time; and the question then stated, was reduced to this short point; Whether the right of Election of the chief officers of this City did belong to the Livery men of the several Companies, with the Lord Maior and Court of Aldermen, by vertue of a Law of this Court, or by vertue of custome.

Mr. Recorder.

I beseech you let it be clear what you go upon.

Mr. *Wildman*.

My Lord I am here desired by many Free-men of this City to appear in their behalf, to inforce a Petition of theirs delivered to this Court; and they also produced to me a Petition preferred by some others in opposition to theirs; And as I conceive, that noble Gentleman Mr. Recorder desires that which is very requisite, that is, that the question may be rightly stated, and so the arguments produced on either side; now I conceive the question is this, Whether the Wardens, Assistants, and Livery men of the severall Companies of this City of *London*, ought to have the Election of the Lord Maior, and Sheriffs of *London*, or whether the Free-men in General by themselves or by their deputies have the right of that Election.

City Counsell.

The question cannot be collected from the Petition, which prays that the people of the several Wards where many forraigners inhabit, may chuse the Lord Maior,

Mr. Wildman.

My Lord, I believe those Gentlemen endeavor so to state the question, that they might make the Court believe that we would split our selves upon that Rock of popular confusion; but we shall endeavor to avoid that clamor. We conceive the question to be this, Whether the Masters, Wardens, Assistants, and Livery men of the several Companies, of right ought to Elect the Lord Maior, and the Sheriffs of this City; Or the Free-men of this City by themselves, or by their deputies. It will be concluded on both sides, that the Lord Maior and Court of Aldermen with the Common Connsel men may have a right in the Election.

City Counsel.

We say the Lord Maior, and the Aldermen. and the Common Counsel, and the Masters, Assistants, and Liveries of the several Companies have the right of the Election, and possession of that right.

Mr. Price.

The question is, whether the Election, as it is, shall continue, or not continue; we deny not that the right of Election doth belong to the Wardens and Livery men of each Company with my Lord Maior and Court of Aldermen. But the question is, whether it belongs to them upon such grounds as are unalterable by this Court; if they are unalterable by this Court, let them shew by what Law; if they are alterable, we are then in a fair way to have one Petition granted.

Mr. Mainard.

There is nothing pretended by the Petition that is endeavored to be made the question. They do complain in their Petition, That this government which you have so long injoyed in this City, is an Imposition of Tyranny and Slavery, and that imposed; when I came first hither, I thought I was to speak to matter of Right, but they decline that, and speak to point of Crime.

Mr. Price.

It is true, these words of Tyranny and Slavery are in the Petition, but they are with a Parenthesis. I desire the Petition may be read.

(The Petition was then read.)

Mr. Price.

We say that the imposition of such and such things is slavery; but it is not in relation to this Court, but in answer to their Petition who call it in their Petition their ancient right; if it be their ancient right, let them shew by what Law; And I conceive the Parenthesis is only in Relation to that expression.

Mr. Wildman.

I humbly conceive (my Lord, and Gentlemen) the thing in question must be collected from the prayer of both Petitions; the sum of the prayer of one Petition is this, that the Representatives of all the Wards may (as of right they ought) elect the chief officers of this City.

Mr. Recorder.

Mr. Recorder.

I think, the business before you, is to come to the question in hand; and I humbly beg, that for expressions on both sides they may be wholly waved; and if you will not speak the question, that you would agree of it in writing.

Mr. Mainard.

I suppose it is conceived by all what we both aim at. I shall be a suitor that those Gentlemen may go on to matter of argument, and I shall speak what I am able.

Mr. Wildman.

May it please your Lordship, to let me pursue the Recorders motion; We humbly conceive that the prayer of our Petition must direct us to state the question; we pray no more but this, that the chief Officers of the City may be chosen by the several Wards in their Representatives annually. We do admit that the Lord Maior, the Court of Aldermen, and Common Counsel may have right of Election, because they represent their Wards; but we pray that our right in Electing, as we are Free-men, may be restored to us.

Mr. Hales.

My Lord, There's no officers of any Corporation in *England*, but are by usage or Charter; and if these Gentlemen be about officers, their question is about the officers of a Corporation; these Gentlemen would introduce some new thing that hath not been heretofore used, and we desire to know upon what imagined pretence they would have it, and that they shew us the persons to inforce the thing they desire; otherwise why do they Petition?

Mr. Wildman.

My Lord, These Gentlemen would aviod the true stating the question, and engage us in Logomachia's, contentions about words; we would know wherein they oppose the desire of our Petition, to have the ancient right of the Citizens of *London* restored to them in the choise of the cheif officers of the City.

Mr. Mainard.

We deny That that you desire in your Petition is the right of the City of *London*. It is so far from being their right, that when they put that in execution, they loose their Charter, and all their Franchises.

Mr. Price.

The question was reduced to this, whether it was in the power of this Court to alter what was then in custome, so that we shall not be lookt upon as adversaries to our Opponents, denying this Court their right of election; but if we make it good, that the custome was altered by you, why then we trust we serve you in so doing, if we prove it in your power to alter it now; and it shall encourage us to pray, and you also to give what we ask, if it shall tend to the good government of this City.

If the right of election belong to the Livery, it must appear by written Law, or by custome time out of minde; if by a Law, it must be by some Law of the Land, or by some Charter, or by some Act of Common hall, or Common Counsel. If it be by Charter, we must insist upon the termes

of

of the Charter, and exponnd the same by succeeding practises, and if this Charter granted in King *Johns* time be meerly declarative, we shall know what the custome was by the succeeding electlons.

If you plead custome, we shall finde custome for many yeers, that the chief Officers of the City were elected by the Lord Maior, Court of Aldermen, Common Counsel men, and the Wards of the City, and not by the Livery men of every Company, as is desired by these Gentlemen.

To the 15. yeer of *Ed.* 4. they are in use from the 19. yeer of *Ed.* the first, which was 194. yeers. It was the practice of the City to choose by Wards so long; And the Aldermen, and Common Counsel men are chosen out of the Wards. Now for election of Maiors and Sheriffs by the Wards, we will give you but a place of that plenty we can give to that purpose, in the 19. yeer of *Ed.* the first 1231. and in the 31. yeer of *Ed.* the first. In the 19 of *Ed.* the first out of twelve men of every Ward, were the Sheriffs chosen; and so was the Maior *Thomas Blun* chosen; the Sheriffs were chosen by the Lord Maior, the Court of Aldermen, and Common Counsel, and twelve men out of every Ward; And *John Lincoln* was so chosen.

And in the 32. of *Ed* the first *John Blun* was so chosen again; and in the 33. of *Ed.* the first, *John Blun* was chosen the 5. time Maior so, and so were the Sheriffs.

And again 1. *Ed.* the second, *Peter Drove* chosen Sheriff as before, and *John Blun* was chosen Maior the sixth time; the first of *Ed.* the second, *Blun* was chosen the seventh time by the Lord Maior, Court of Aldermen, & the Community which was summoned thereunto, which was twelve men out of every Ward; and in the 2. of *Ed.* the second, *Bucler* and *Dover* were chosen Sheriffs as before; the time would fail if we should speak of *Palmer* and *Edmonds*, &c. and many others who were chosen by the Lord Maior, the Aldermen, the Common Counsel, and the good men of Wards.

At the 22. yeer of *Henry* the sixth, were present at election of the Maior all the Common Counsel men, and several discreet Citizens chosen out of every Ward; its true they are called the Commons and Community, and if that you look in the 21. of *Ed.* the first, the Community there is expounded to be the honest, discreet, and wise men of the Ward; so that they were Representatives chosen out of the the Wards; but if it be objected, that besides these twelve honest discreet men of every Ward, there were certain other men that did belong unto this election, and surely it may imply that the Livery men did belong unto the election; surely. no; but by those dark expressions, must be meant the honest discreet men chosen out of the Wards with the Lord Maior and Aldermen, to whom it belongs *ex officio*.

The main argument was this; That the chief Officers of the City were to be chosen by the Lord Maior, and the Aldermen, and Sheriffs, and the Common Counsel men, with twelve men chosen out of every Ward that were discreet men, that was granted; but that they were such discreet men, as to exclude others, was denyed:

If that these are the men, they must be distinguished from other men by another term then discreet men. Now you argue thus, that Livery men are discrete: & therefore the men that must chose my Lord Maior, are the Livery men : as if you should argue, That the LordMaior wears a golden Chain, therefore the Sheriffs are Lord Majors, because they wear golden Chains.

I Humbly offer these Considerations :

1. My Lord Maior, nor the Aldermen chuse not any officers of the Companies; why should they then chuse any chief Officers of the City?

Secondly, The jurisdiction of the Major and Sheriffs extends to a Local Power; and by these Gentlemens pleading, Livery men, Free of this City, may live at *York*; and if they be at *London* that day my Lord Major is chosen, they may choose my Lord Major and the Sheriffs of this City, and yet live not under their Power.

Thirdly, The way of election we plead for, doth not exempt them from being chosen by the Ward to elect.

Fourthly, Free-men of this City pay Shot and Lot, and are bound to assist the chief Officers of this City : but Livery men living not under these bounds, are not under this obligation.

Fifthly, Again, this City is distributed by way of Wards; Questmen, Jury-men, Constables, and Scavengers are all chosen by the Wards; and it is most necessary for the well Government of this City, that the chief Officers of this City be chosen by Representatives from every Ward.

Sixthly, If there be any miscariage in Government, The Citizens living in the City must be taxt, and pay any fine for misgovernment, and therefore it is most fit they should have their vote in election.

Seventhly, and further, if any accident happen by Fire or the miscariage of one or more of the chief Officers, if it so fall out that the Treasure of the Chamber should be exhausted and miss-imployd, the Orphans cannot have their portions, I desire to know who must be responsible for it; the Livery men of the several Companies, or the whole Wards, and every particular man thereof ?

And here give me leave to be heard with Charity : God knows my Heart, I speak out of Love to you all, and as prest in Conscience; what I have to say, I am sure it is the whisperings, nay the Report of most, and I fear too true; That the cry of the Fatherless and the Widdow doth sollicite Heaven for vengeance, for the expending the poor Orphanes Estates; and we trust and believe, that your Honor and this Honorable Court, whose Faces, and Lives, and Conversations we so well know, that we do verily believe that your Hearts and Hands are clean from this pollution; but as we do believe, so we hope, that your Honor and the rest will take some speedy course that the blood of the Fatherless and the Widdow may not stick to these walls; Let our blood and Estates go before the blood of poor Orphans, that that may not one day be charged upon this City. I desire to be pardoned this digression.

I

I should answer some objections that are commonly made against this way of election that we desire: The first is this, That this will destroy the Companies, and so at last it will strike higher, to wit, the overthrow of my Lord Major and the Court of Aldermen, and so consequently all Government; for my part, I know not that *Absolon* among us, but did I know such a man, my Hand should be upon him as soon as any mans; I say let a Bear robbed of her whelps meet me, rather then a People without Government; the Magistrates power is my power, and is in him for my use, and for my part I am for the Majesty of Magistrats: for when we read of Kings, we read of Thrones and Scepters, and soft raiment. &c.

It is true, though your chians are gold, yet they are chains as well as gold: and though your Gowns be Honorable, yet they are burdensome as well as Honorable.

But as for the business in hand, we speak not against the Form and the beauty of it but let every Star shine in his own Orbe.

Let there be no confusion; let Wards have their dues, and let Companies have their dues; I want opportunity to set forth their glory and their excellency in their proper places. As for the objections of popularity and confusion, we shall answer them if they be insisted on.

Mr. *Wildman*.

My Lord, I humbly propose no other end, but to inforce the Petition of the Free-men of this City: the question that was stated is this, Whether the Companies of the several Mysteries in the City, or the Free-men in the several Wards have right to choose the Lord Major and the Sheriffs. Now it rests upon us to prove, that the Free-men in their Representatives, chosen out of the Wards, are to choose; and we do assert this for a truth, That those, and those only that shall be actually chosen to represent the Free-men of the City of *London*, not excluding the Lord Major, Court of Aldermen, and Common Counsel, have a right to this election. And to make this right of the Free-men of the City apparent, I might according to the practise of some, urge no more but Common and natural right, those very foundations of Common Right which the Parliament have declared to us; I mean the first principles of just Government.

As first, that all just subjection of a People unto Governours ought to proceed from consent of parties: or,

Secondly, that all officers or Governours are but trustees for the good of the People, and therefore are to receive their trust from the people, none having Power under God to invest a trust of Government in any but the people, nor to set the Bounds and Limits of the trust of several Governors; and this the Parliament hath declared to us, *viz.* That the original of all just power under God proceeds from the People.

And my Lord, I might insist upon it, that this very City and Common Councel in all things do acknowledge this to be the Peoples Right; For upon your election of your Representatives in Parliament, the Commissions you give them run in the name of the whole Commonalty of the City. And it is generally admitted to be the peoples right in all Acts of Common Counsel and other publick Acts, which run in the name of the Commonalty of the City, they are therefore supposed to do those Acts by themselves or deputyes: But, my Lord, I shall wave this, left I should reduce all Government to an uncertainty, by dissolving it into the first principles, and so seem at least to run upon that Rock of confusion which those Gentlemen would have us split our selves upon; But it is no way our intention, and therefore I shall assert this proposition; That the Representers of the several Wards ought to chuse the Lord Major and the Sheriffs upon a Right declared by written Law; only I crave leave to premise, or to inform this Honorable Court, that those first Records that should make out the peoples right, are imbezeled, burnt or lost, there being no Record in your Treasury but since *Ed.* 1. For it hath been the practise of several Kings to purloyn the Records that they might with more facility incroach upon the peoples rights; As I remember it was an Article against King *Richard* the second, that he had purloyned and destroyed the ancient Records.

But my Lord, by Records that are extant, the Liberties of the Citizens of London appear to be more ancient then any Charter of the City thats visible to us: in the 9. Chap. of *Magna Charta* it is said, *The City of London shall have all her Liberties and Customes she was used to have;* so that there were Liberties and Customes that the City had before the great Charter of *England*. Now it is agreed by the Gentlemen of the long Robe, that the great Charter of *England* is chiefly declarative of the Common Law; And Sir *Edward Cook* in his second part of his Institutes upon that ground declares it for Law, that Any Law made by the Parliament it self, and contrary to the great Charter of *England*, and contrary to right reason, is voyd of it self.

I suppose he addes these words [And contrary to right reason] to shew that he means only that a Statute made against that part of the great Charter which is declarative of the Common Law, is null of it self; for the Common Law, being right reason, it cannot be supposed without a contradiction, that Parliaments should of right have power to make a Law against Right. Now the Liberties of *London* being confirmed by the great Charter, I cannot conceive that any other Liberties are there intended to be confirmed, then those common Liberties that were grounded upon right reason, and then those words of the ninth Chapter of the great Charter do but declare the Common Law, and by consequence are unalterable; and any Law made against those Liberties of *London* either by a Power within the City, or without the City, is null of it self; now to make it appear that it was one of the City Liberties before the great Charter, that the Free-men should chuse their chief officers, we can go no farther

then

then your Charter granted by King *John*, in the year (1215) 435. years since; that is the first Charter the City of *London* hath extant. And by that Charter tis said to be granted to the Barons of *London* yearly to elect a Major and Sheriffs, and the word Barons doth import no more then the Free-men of *London*; for then the Free-men of every port were called Barons, though since it hath been made a name and title of honor peculiar to those called Noblemen. Now I conceive it will be agreed by the Gentlemen of the other side that this very Charter was not the original of those Liberties of *London* that are mentioned there to be granted, but that it was only declarative, shewing what the Liberties of the City were; and here I must infer, that this Charter declaring that the Barons of the City (wherein every particular Citizen is included) should chuse the Major and the Sheriffs, this (I say) doth but declare what was the Common right of all the Citizens of *London* before this Charter.

I may then from hence conclude, that before the great Charter it was the right of the Citizens of *London*, none excluded, that they should chuse their Major and their Sheriffs; and such a right as I crave leave to affirm to be unalterable, that is justly so; for being a right by the Law of nature, 'tis superior to all other Laws; and other Laws are only so far right, as they agree with that; however I may more boldly say, that this Libertie of the Citizens of *London* being confirmed by the great Charter, cannot be null by an act of Common Councel; and I humbly conceive that it was not in the Common Counsels Power to make that act in the fifteenth of *Edward* the fourth to debar all but the Liveries of the several Companies to come to the election of the Major, and Sheriffs: for they could not take away the right of the Citizens declared by their Charter; and in the first Charter, and all others tis said to be granted to the Citizens indefinitely, to chuse of themselves a Major: and the Charter ought to be construed in favour of right, and so tis to be taken that tis granted to all the Citizens: and this their right is apparent by the use of it which is mentioned in all the most ancient Records of the City: there's one or two very clear to this purpose. The City growing great and very populous after their first Charters, found it unconvenient to meet together, the Commonalty being very great: and therefore according to this their right which we assert, the whole City at a Common hall did make an agreement that 8. 10. or 12. of every Ward should be chosen by their Wards, and in their names and in their steads elect the Major and the Sheriffs of the City.

As in the sixth year of *Edward* the second Lib. D. Folio 3. which if you please I desire may be Read, that you may not think I speak without book. The Act was read.

And in the 20. year of *Edward* the third, in the year 1347. there is an Act of a Common Hall recorded, wherein tis said that there gathered together on *Simon* and *Ludes* day the whole Commonalty into Guild Hall

C

London,

London, so that the whole Hall was full with the Communalty.

The Act read in those words.

And it is agreed that from henceforth there shall come the Major, the Aldermen, and also out of every Ward of the City of London 12. 8. *or.* 6. *According as the ward shall be great or small, of the richest and wisest of every Ward; and such* 12 8. *or.* 6. *with the Major and Aldermen shall intermeddle and chuse a Major and Sheriffs for the year following.* I conceive this is sufficient to prove that it is the Citizens of Londons right to chuse the Major and Sheriffs of *London*; for accordingly they did meet together, the whole Body of the Free-men; and finding that inconvenient, the commonalty did agree at a full Hall, that such a select number should be chosen by every Ward, and sent to the election of the Maior and Sheriffs, as appeares by the Act that hath been read; & tis probable, that this was not the first time that such an agreement was made, but that this was made after the Commonalty had upon some occasion reassumed the power of electing to themselves; for according to this agreement it was the practice of the City of *London* for neer two hundred yeers before it was put into the hands of the Liverymen of each Company; in 19. *Ed.* the first, *lib. c. fol.* 62. the election of the Maior and Sheriffs, is said to have been made by the Maior, Sheriffs and Aldermen, and twelve men of every Ward.

In the 19. yeer of *Ed.* the first, *Blun* was chosen Maior of the City of *London*, by the Common Counsel and Aldermen, and by the assent of twelve honest men of every Ward of the whole City.

My Lord, It is apparent that twelve men were chosen by every Ward, that did elect the Lord Maior and the Sheriffs. And the very same words are in the 31. yeer of *Ed.* 1. where *Martin* and *Burford* were chosen Sheriffs; and in the 32. of *Ed.* the first where *John Blun* was so chosen Maior. *lib. c. fol.* 111. & 112. and in the first yeer of *Ed.* the second *fol.* 112. *Picot* and *Dury* were so chosen Sheriffs. I humbly submit it to your Lordship, whether you will see these Records. I may quote more, as in the third of *Ed.* 2. *l. c. in fol.* 113. *&c.* It was the continual practice from yeer to yeer, that the twelve men chosen by every Ward, did elect the Lord Maior, and the Sheriffs; there is a whole Jury of witnesses in the Records to this purpose. And my Lord, where this usage may seem to have ceased, because in other Records tis said they were elected by the Lord Maior, Sheriffs, and Aldermen, and the whole Commonalty; we shall make it appear that this is meant the selected men of the Wards; though however those Records are clear for us: for if the choice was by the whole Commonalty, it was either by themselves, or these deputies. Yet we find one Record in the 21. of *Ed.* the first, *lib. c. fol.* 6. where tis said, first that there was assembled the whole Commonalty, and

and then tis explained in thefe words, that is to fay of every Ward the richeft and the wifeft.

The Record was read.

Mr. *Wildman*.

I produce this Record for this end, to fhew that where the election is faid to be by the Commonalty of the City, it is to be underftood the felect number of every Wards Reprefentatives; for it is fuppofed every one is included; and therefore tis faid to be by the Commonalty. I pray my Lord obferve thefe words in this Record, *the whole Commonalty, that is to fay the more able and difcreet men of every ward.* And to confirm this, if there be any need of it, we can produce another Record in 113 *fol. libro* C. Where election is faid to be made by the Commonalty fummoned thereunto: yet in *Pag.* 112. of the fame, it is faid men of every Ward did chufe: whence I collect that by the expreffion of the Commonalty fumoned hereto, is underftood the twelve men from the Wards; fo that it appeareth clearly in my humble opinion, that it was the practice of the City for neer two hundred yeers to choofe by their Reprefentatives, before it came to be the ufage of the City to chufe by the Livery men of the Companies.

And my Lord, if it were needful to ftrengthen this, we can fhew by * Records that Parliament men were chofen by the Lord Maior, Aldermen, and twelve men of every Ward; thefe were the Reprefenters of the Wards, that joyned with the Lord Maior, and the Court of Aldermen in fuch elections; And the Commiffions given to the Parliament men, are in the name of the whole Commonalty of the City, which admits they were all there in their perfons or in their deputies, to chufe them, and give them their Commiffions: elfe the Commonalty is abufed in having their names ufed in the Commiffions.

* *Lib.C.fo.*41¾ *Edw.* I.

Now my Lord, I fhall take the boldnefs to conclude from all this evIdence, of the Common Counfel of *London*, though I much honor their power, and would be infinitely loth to detract from it: yet my Lord I muft crave leave to affirm, That it being the liberty of all the Free-men of *London*, by themfelves or deputies, to chufe the Lord Maior and Sheriffs; And this being confirmed to them by *Magna Charta*, as unalterable: And all the people having declared at a ful Common Hall. that they had put it into the hands of twelve men which were their deputies, or Reprefentatives to elect the chief officers of this City; this my Lord being the Cafe, I fay, I humbly affirm, that it was not in the power of the Common Counfel by that Act 15.E 4 to take away the Free-mens right, nor to fay who fhould be the peoples deputies to make their elections, they

they being by the people deputies themselves, & deputed to another power; So that my Lord, I now conclude that it was the ancient undoubted right of the Citizens of *London* by themselves or their deputies, to make their election of their Maior and Sheriffs, and other chief officers of the City; and I conceive the Petition of the Freemen of the City of *London*, which I now endeavor to inforce, amounts to no more then a modest humble claim of their Common right, that elections might for future be made by the deputies of every Ward, which was the ancient custome of the City before the great Charter; and all their Charters, that of King *John*, and since, say that the election shall be according to the ancient custom of the City.

Mr. *Wildman*.

And if the King at any time sent Writs, or made Proclamations for quieting the elections when there was disturbances, and prohibited the accefs of people: Yet the more honest and difcreet men of the several Wards are mentioned as bound to come to the election, and tis commanded that they chufe *prout moris est*, according to their cuftome; and I conceive it hath been proved that it was their cuftome to chufe by the Reprefentatives of every Ward. I shall say nothing for the conveniency of this way of choice that I plead for, becaufe we claim it as our right: and we expect that the Arguments againft us will be chiefly from pretended inconveniences; and when thofe arguments are produced, we shall endeavor to anfwer them.

Mr. *Maynard*.

I fuppofe to fatisfie your confciences what is the right in that which is indeavored by thefe gentlemen to be defended, which they have taken very great pains about, in collecting what hath been faid to you; I shall endeavor Gentlemen in the first place to remove that which feemeth to lie in my way, and fo come to that which I have to fay in anfwer to what hath been fpoken by you.

The Gentleman that firft fpake, taking occafion to make an apology for his own unability to perform the work in his hands, he was pleafed to fay that which I conceive you do not believe; he would make as if he wanted parts, when certainly he fhewed very great skill in the very entrance of the bufinefs; and when the fact was but a litle ftated, he wonld have laid hold of you all, and fo of making you Judges, he would have made you Parties; And indeed it is well that you are both Judges and Parties;

they

they said, and doubtlefs they are ingenious, that they defire you to proceed according as you should be fatisfied in confcience, the which for my part I doubt not but that you will; there was much faid how much it did behove you in point of danger; but what that danger is I underftand not; but he tels you he urged it out of zeal; alfo he tels you much of fome fecret *Abfolon*; but for my part, I underftand not what, nor who he means hereby; I will take no advantage of any mans affections nor inclinations at all; But the main which that Gentleman fpake to the bufinefs in hand, was that he cited many precedents and records for the practice of what he now defireth may be effected; But truly I do extreamly much mifunderftand thofe prefidents and Records that he produceth, If that they are not as full againft them, as any thing can be faid.

I shall firft offer the weight of their reafons which they urge without prefident; which deals moft candidly, you shall judge; for I shall involve the former in the latter, Mr. *Price* in Mr. *Wildman*; and firft that that was urged by Mr. *Wildman* by way of reafon was this, that it is a principle of Common right, that juft fubjection cannot be but by affent, and there is no way whereby this affent may be but this he fpeaks of. I do deny his Major. I shall deny his firft propofition; there is, and may be juft fubjection without affent; and certainly the experience of all generations in the world evidences this truth, that there may be juft fubjection without affent; and there be but few governments but are eftablished without affent: it is true, where the affent is, the eafier is the fubjection born. But what doth he mean by affent? a virtual or perfonal affent? if he means perfonal affent, why then when should there be any fuch affent? but to fay no man nor people shalbe governed but by affent, we deny; for is not a lawful conqueft a lawful title in fome Cafes? the matter is not to make the bufinefs impoffible without affent. But to that which they deliver, I can no way affent. He tels you that the feveral Wards muft have Reprefentatives to elect the cheif officers of this City, and he tels you the firft Records were loft and imbezeled; But it is not right placed.

But Gentlemen, what doth he conclude? he tels you there were Records, and he tels you without all queftion, if that they were extant, they would fpeak for them; although he nor none elfe know the contents of them. But faith he, the Liberties of *London* are Ancienter then the great Charter, and the Liberties of *London* being confirmed by that Law; therefore any Law made againft that, is voyd and null; and therefore the Common Counfel cannot change them.

Mr. Wildman.

I said that wherein the great Charter was declarative of the Common Law, *i.e.* right reason, it was unalterable; and any Liberty of *London* of that nature, such as is that we now plead for, ought also to be unalterable.

Mr. Mainard.

You said this, that our City Liberties are ancienter then *Magna Charta*, and that they are confirmed by *Magna Charta*, and therefore cannot be altered by any Law, much less by the Common Counsel.

I shall appeal to the whole Auditory for the Argument; then what ever *Magna Charta* hath confirmed, cannot be by any Law repealed; and when this comes to generals, this may be of very sad consequence; I see Laws are edged tools; those that understand them, make good use of them: and those that do not understand them, will finde that they are sharpe, and will cut; we all know that there were Bishops and Kings by the Common Law, and *Magna Charta*, and yet they are changed, and justly changed by the Parliament: and you will not say that that is void and and null, &c. Now he comes to the presidents which I did tell you before, and hope to make it clear, that the presidents cited do otherthrow that which they bring them for. I shall offer unto you, that which according to the best of my Judgement, is matter of reason, and proof of that which hath been affirmed by them. I shall not beg any favor from you, in regard I speak for that which is dear to you all, which is the peace, prosperity and well Government of this famous City: we shall first lay before you the fact, and from thence proceed to the question. From the fifteenth of *Edward* the fourth, there hath been a succession of Election this way, and that cannot be denyed by any, which is nigh two hundred yeers. If any man lay claim to any thing, he either doth claim of right, or prescription.

Now if a man should come and put you to prove your right, when you have had possession of an estate 150. yeers past, you would think your self hardly dealt withall. Now we shall prove that there hath been 180. yeers possession of election this way, and it hath by the blessing of God brought with it peace, prosperity, and plenty to you; and I hope you are not so ungrateful, but to acknowledge it; but it is

told

told you, and much pains is taken to perſwade you by theſe gentlemen that this muſt be removed; but under favour upon little grounds.

You ſee here are but two, and theſe two differ in what they would maintain. Now all Truths ſtand one with another; ſaith one, this is lawful; ſaith another, this cannot be changed; either you muſt conclude the preſent is lawful or unlawful; if lawful, why is it deſired to be changed? but judge you the conſequents of this; if you deny this way now eſtabliſht to be lawful, then the whole City of *London* for above two hundred yeers never had one lawful Maior, and all Actions proformed by them may be queſtioned. Now in the fourty one of Queen *Elizabeth*, there being a difference in the City about election of officers, all the Judges of *England* were cauſed to meet together about this very thing; and it was expreſly reſolved by them all, that ſuch elections were lawful, and *London* is named in the reſolution; and it is ſaid they found it a queſtion of very great advice, and thoſe Judges were very grave, pious, and godly men, for ſome of them, as *Popham* and *Anderſon*, and *Pyriam* alſo a famous man; ſo that gentlemen, fifty yeers agoe this queſtion was on foot, and all the Judges of the Land did then give their reſolutions, that it would be matter of very great inconveniency to alter it, and they gave it as in right of Law to belong, as it had been before; and if it be not lawful, then this City hath forfeited its Charter, and is lyable, when they that are above in power and authority at any time ſhall be pleaſed, to be queſtioned for it; I do apprehend that the foundation of your right doth not depend upon any Charter; thoſe Charters you have, are matter of confirmation, and not Charters that do give you your right; the ancienteſt Record that you produce, is from King *John*, but the firſt yeer of *Richard* the firſt is the utmoſt bounds of memory. If that it be not by preſcription, why then are many cuſtoms of the City void? for there are many cuſtomes and uſages for which there is no Charter, nor is it poſſible there ſhould be; and therefore it muſt of neceſſity follow, that Maiors was time out of mind; and the truth is, Maiors were in uſe before the Charter; they were indeed called Portwards and Portriſts; but the name was changed in *Richard* the firſt's time, and from thence they were called Maiors, and the Charter was granted in the name of the Maior; ſo that though the officers name be changed, it is the ſame officer ſtill, the power the ſame, but not the name, if they were not by cuſtome; for you muſt know what is by cuſtome, is not by Charter, and what is by Charter is not by cuſtome. Now then what is the Charter? the Barons of themſelves may chooſe a Maior; this Charter being of this Antiquity, it ſhall be conſtrued according to uſage, and that is a rule in Law, and that is your conſequence; for if we ſhall be forced to finde out the meaning of words, you will be to ſeek; for Citizens in thoſe times were called

Barons.

Barons. But we shall now come to answer their objections, and to make those objections we have to say on the other side. Those Records that they produce, say, we shall all choose, and if that you hold your selves to the letter, then you are tyed to an impossibility, that is every Cittizen, none excluded, and then you will reduce your selves to an absolute impossibility; but say they, we would have a Representative made out of every Ward, and so they with the Maior and Court of Aldermen, should choose the cheif officers of the City; but this doth no more stand as an objection against the present choice; for if you look to the words of the Record produced, it doth not bear it; for doth the Charter grant you any such Representative? Taking it for granted, the right is founded upon Charter, and not upon custome: and I take it to be by ancient custom before the Charter, or else the Charter would not bear it, that they should choose a Maior, and not telling them how and when; for this general grant was made because it was their custom; but an objection is made, that in this way which we now choose, all do not choose. But I answer; all do choose, though not by their own votes; you say, when did we give our right to the Livery men to give vote for us? I answer a man seeth with the eye, yet we say the man seeth; a mans hand moveth, but it is the man that moveth it; so though every part doth not do every thing in the City, yet the whole doth every thing, and the City doth choose, though every member thereof be not at the choice; so that the question is whether you do believe this was lawfully done by those that do it. Now if Lawfully, why then they are the Cities Representatives; as for example, for the Parliament, every member thereof cannot give his vote for the passing of all things: for many times, many of them are in the Country when many Acts are past, and yet we say the Parliament doth it; as in election of Parliament men in the Country, the Writs run, that the people shall choose; and yet we all know that none choose but such as are Free-holders, although there may be many as good men as Freeholders, yet they have no vote: and yet this act is accounted the Act of all the Commons in *England*, though they come in but by some parts, and some have no vote in the choice of them; we may not depart from this; for by this we hold all we have; so if this be a lawful choice, why then the Law supposes that where there is a continuance of a lawful possession, there all lawful meanes is supposed to maintain the possession.

It

If that all the City should meet together, and set down this Order; if that it be once setled, that for ever hereafter these and these shall chuse; then you make those your Trustees, and it supposeth such an ancient custom was. And truely, Gentlemen, the choice as now it is, is no otherwise: for the Aldermen they are chosen by the Ward, and so are the Common Councel.

I will put you a Case, which, to my understanding, is like this. In the 28 yeer of *Edward* the first, there was a Statute made, wherein the King grants to the People, that they shall chuse the Sheriffs, or conservators of the Peace; whenas there was nothing more clear, that none but the Free-holders should chuse them. Mark the Parallel; and yet this is an Act of Parliament that hath its beginning at that time: and yet that is accounted the choice of the People.

I shall now come to examine that which I told you of, the presidents which they produced; which I was bold to tell you, that every one of them made against them.

That which is desired is, That every Ward should chuse them Representatives, and that those Representatives, together with my Lord Maior and Court of Aldermen, should chuse the chief Officers of the City. And in proof to this, I shall appeal to your Memories, and to the words of the Presidents, whether one President that they produce, prove, that those six, eight, or twelve men that were summoned to chuse, were chosen by the Ward. You shall see what a pass you will come to, if you go according to their meaning of those Presidents. Says the first President, *They were summoned from each Ward*. They did not summon themselves. Pray then who summoned them? Why it was the Maior that summoned them: the Maior summoned whom he would; sometimes six, sometimes eight, sometimes twelve, at his pleasure; and he summoned sometimes the Honest men, sometimes the Rich men, and sometimes the Wise men; and they came and made election of the Maior. There is not the least tittle in all the Records that they produce, that they were chosen by the Ward. It is one thing to say, Twelve men that were summoned from such a Ward, came; and another thing to say, Twelve men that were elected by the Ward, came and chose: and yet so it is said, that at that Convention there should be six, eight, or twelve of the Honestest, Wisest, and Richest men of the Ward chose.

If that there should be such a Summons sent out, That all the Richest and all the Wisest of such and such a Ward should come, what a kinde of Summons is this! and how shall you judge of these persons? *&c.*

But it appeares the Maior sent out his Process and summoned them, and so a Law is made, that none should come but those who are thus summoned: as it appeares, in the election of *Blunn*, Maior, and all along no mention made of electing the persons, but summoning them to appear.

J: D

Other-

Otherwise this must be understood to be the Common Councel of the City of *London*, for they have had several tearmes; and a man may very well say, when the right is in the Commons to do this, or that, that when it is done by their Trustee, it is done by the Commons. Now the Common Councel are often so called, the Commons of the City. Now how will you understand that these six, eight, or twelve men were onely chosen for this end, To chuse the chief Officers? There is nothing less in the * Record: onely Master *Wildman* fancies that the Ward meet upon this occasion, and elected them; and then the Maior should summon them. So that, I say; there could not be stronger presidents then what they have produced, that make against themselves. I shall now conclude what inconveniences would follow in point of Law, in case they had their desire.

2 Edw. 1.
fol. 41.

Secondly, You put your selves upon this hazard, that if you part from that which is warranted by Charter, and warranted by the possession of two hundred yeers, and warranted by the Resolution of those twelve Judges; I say, Then you will forfeit your Charter which you have so long enjoyed.

Thirdly, It will be inconvenient to you, in regard of your Liberty in the Ancient Laws of *England*. No man dwelt in any Ward, but was sworn to appear upon all Summons to Courts.

Your Wards have Courts of Inquest: and over them, you have the Sheriffs Court; and this Court, which is above that: and no man can line out of those Jurisdictions.

Your Wards in the City, are like your Hundred-Courts in the Country. And heretofore, in all Wards, every one was to be summoned; assoon as one was twelve yeers old, they were to be summoned, to give an account of their life.

In a Ward, you know, there are many that are not Free-men; and there are many Free-men that have their habitations abroad. Now if you admit of all to come to choice, why then Forreiners that live in the Ward, shall have more freedom then Free-men which live out of the Ward; and it may so fall out, that in some Wards there may be more Strangers then Free-men. So that in this way of choice by the Ward, oftentimes those that are Citizens may be excluded, and those that are Forreiners may be included.

But you may say, We will exclude those that are not Free-men from choice. But was there ever any such thing done in this world?

The next thing that will follow it, will be this, Popularity. Gentlemen, you must remember that I told you that the Ward consisteth of every inhabitant thereof: and when you are in such a populous place as this City is, and when that they shall all meet together, what breaches of Peace and Insurrections may come! I speak not of that which is without president: and such Meetings cannot be, in any wise mans apprehension, but this will follow. But

But truely I do not look upon this as the greatest danger; but there is this in it also: The foundation upon which this is grounded, which the Doctrinal part of the Law, in this case is undermined, and the example of such a thing as this. For after this example, truely all the Government or Corporations of this Kingdom will receive such shakings, as I blush to mention, when they shall consider the Ancient Government of this City, so backt with Lawful authority, put into a new way. There is not a more dangerous thing, in my understanding.

Heretofore, when the Prerogative did lie upon you, you did shew your selves constant to your own Interest. Truely, this is a meer designe to betray you; and it will shake you all to pieces, if you look not to it: for it is an earth quake under you, and will blowe you up.

As for that Principle M. W. asserted concerning just Subjection, because he left it, lest he should reduce things to an uncertainty, I shall say nothing: onely I shall briefly lay down 1. wherein we are agreed, 2. wherein we differ.

M. *Hayles*.

My Lord and Gentlemen,

First, It is agreed to by them, that the power of the choice of my Lord Maior is not meerly by Charter, but by Prescription too; That the Charter is a Confirmation, and not the Original: For we do say, that there was the same Office of Maior many yeers before King *John*: so that your Officers of the City have been time out of minde, and not barely by the Charter. And if it were not so, that would overthrow all your Courts and Franchises.

Secondly, This is agreed to on both sides, that without all question the Common Councel shall have a Vote in election of the Maior: in this we agree. But the Dispute is, Whether or no the Livery and Assistants of the Companies shall come in with their Voice, or whether there shall be a new Device, that the Citizens shall meet and chuse twelve men of each Ward; as they do in the choice of the Common Councel; and so they shall elect the Maior.

Thirdly, We agree in this, that is, that the way of Election hath been by the Maior, Aldermen, Common Councel, and Livery-men, and hath been used for about One hundred and eighty yeers. And they affirm that this was grounded upon an Act of Common Councel.

These three things are agreed unto on both sides.

But now the great heat is against the Livery-men; and the reasons they give against them, are these three.

First, They argue from point of inconveniency. That is, because the Maior and Aldermen, do not choose the Masters and Wardens of the Companies, therefore they should not choose the Maior, and Officers of the City.

The second Reason they give, is in point of right. I shall say no

No more of that then what hath been said already: You have had a choice of Maior, and Sheriffes, for neer two hundered years, by the Aldermen, Common Councel, and Livery, to argu-election out of convenicncie that you have been under two hundred yeers. To al.er the it upon M. Prises opinion, I think you will not, you having found it every way so convenient and profitable to y u.

But if so be there be any inconveniency in this, a popular choice will be very much more inconvenient. I pray consider but this one thing: If so be the people should come hereafter, and dispute the validity of this choyce you plead for, and say, What do you tell us of Representatives! we will all choose our selves; What imaginary grounds can there be to say, These feares are but imaginary? How will it be, when it will come to be thus? They will say, We will go and chuse a Maior our selves; there is nothing of Right in this, but meerly maginations: if you allow of ten, or twelve, they may say, Why not fi'ty, or a hundred, or two hundred? But for point of right, you have heard what hath been said upon these three heads.

But saith M. *Wildman*, the foundation of all power is in the People first: If that shall be a ground to let in all the generality of Citizens into an actual choice of Officers, will there not be the same reason for Apprentices, and Forreigners, to plead for Votes in your Election? A Forreigner is under the power of the Maior, and Apprentices live under the command of the Maior.

The next Reason is, they would endeavour to prove that this course of Election they plead for, was heretofore usual. I shall say but two words to that.

First, they insist upon the Charter, and that of King *John*: the words are, *They shall Elect a Maior.*

And they produce some Presidents of the one and thirtieth of *Edward* the first, and the first of *Edward* the second.

I shall repeate one word or two of that my brother *Maynard* omitted.

First, you will remember we proved a constant usage of neer two hundred yeers in this way of Election; and their pretence is but for a few certaine yeers, that the choice was in that way which they desired.

A second thing shewes their pitiful mistake. The Common-Councel are agreed to have a choice: why if they examine it, they will finde, the Common-Councel are men chosen by the Ward. They do finde here and there mention made, that the Maior was chosen by the Aldermen, and about six, eight, or twelve men summoned. And here they think, that they must needs be Representatives chosen by the Ward; whenas in truth, these might very well be the Common Councel of the Ward.

I think there is nothing left for me to say to that. What I shall offer, shall be out of Record, and never mention the conveniencies nor

incon-

Inconveniencies. I shall read the Records unto you, that they produce; and I will take hold of some words of them. The words are these: **There shall come out of every Ward twelve, eight, or six men,** according to the greatness of the Ward. And according to the Wards of *London* the Common Councel men were sent, some more, and some less. And this is very obvious, that where there is such a description of the number for each Ward, there must needs be meant the Common Councels. So that of necessity these words extend to the Common Councel-men, or else the Common Councel must be excluded.

And again, from a Record *Edw* 3 they argue the Commonalty to be the twelve men, when they are the Liveries. So they mistake in their application.

We are not to dispute who may alter the Custom: But they say, This is your Custom, and they say That is.

We will admit, that that which is by a Fundamental Law or Charter, cannot be altered by an Act of Common Councel. But if your present choice be not lawful, then all bargains made since *Edw.* 1. by your Officers, are void, and you have no power to judge: for you are no Common Councel.

M. *Prise.*

I humbly conceive I may answer him to what hath been objected against what I delivered according to Reason. You say that I did declare that just subjection cannot be but by assent. Under favour, that was not offered by me. But I affirm, that just subjection cannot be but by right of assent.

Secondly, They urge that we differ upon our grounds. The one saith that it is lawful, the other saith not. And the Reason is, because they that grant it have no power to grant it. But for my part, I did not assert any such thing.

As concerning the resolution of the Judges that you so much speak of; In some cases it is considerable, and in some cases little weight is to be given to their Resolutions. For we all know, in the case of Ship-money, they gave in their Resolutions, that it was according to Law. And we also know, that this was afterwards condemned by the Parliament, to be contrary to Law, and Illegal.

Secondly, The Resolutions of those very Judges you so much extoll, doth no way refer to the business.

We offer to grant a select number may lawfully choose; but the Liveries are not so. And the opinion of the Judges onely say, that a select number may choose.

Thirdly, Whereas it is said, the Charter is Declarative,

To that I Answer,

The Practice succeeding doth declare what the Custome then was; and we have no mention of any Masters, or Livery-men of Compa-

M. Wild spake last for the City-Liveries, to the same purpose as the other: He had no new Argument; onely an observation from 28 Edw.1.

nies in Election. And for expofition of the Charter, if that we tie you to the Letter of it, you fay we tie you to an impoffibility. But we onely plead for the Reprefent tves of Wards, to chufe not all perfonally: and therein is no impoffibility.

Fol. 6. li. C.

And befides, in the one and twentieth of *Edward* the firft, it is expounded what was meant by thofe words.

We proved the Charter gave it the City, and the City gave it the Common Councel, and the Common Councel gave it to the L very; and if they gave it for good, if they finde it prejudicial ye may take it away againe.

Whereas they fay that by the Number of fix, eight, or ten, is doubtlefs meant the Common Councel; How do you prove the Common Councel-men did confift of fo many in every Ward?

And then for the Expofition of the Ward Moat: Whereas they fay fome Forreigners may chufe; yea they may infer as well, Forreigners may be chofen.

To that I anfwer, many men may be fummoned together about bufinefs, and fome of them may have a right to fome things there in hand, and fome may not.

We have a prefident, once one that was no Freeman, was chofen to be a Sheriffe of *London*; and becaufe he was no Freeman, therefore the Election was Null. So though it be granted, that every particular man of every Ward, be fummoned to come to the Ward-Moat; yet it doth not follow that he hath a right to all the work to be done in that Court. Again, for the Popularity and Confequences which they fo much plead, that will every whit reflect upon this honourable Court. For every member of this Honourable Court is chofen by that party which they call Popular: therefore let them fpeak of that till to morrow morning, all will reflect upon you. That which is now pleaded for, is Cuftome.

Thirdly, That this hath been the Practice for a hundered and eighty years, I do not deny; but I do not grant it. Suppofe we do grant it, and yet we bring a Practice for within twelve years, that was another Practice; whether an intermiffion of Practices do not rend that which is called Cuftome, I humbly offer. For my part, I did not offer the Argument of Conveniency in Relation to the prefent Practice; but according to this Principle I argue againft the unreafonablenefs of this Priviledge, that thefe Gentlemen would have to this right, and not by Authority of this Court. Againe they fay, that if Election be by the Ward, men will plead thus: Why not fifty or a hundred, as well as fix, eight or twelve?

Again they urge, that Livery men were called the Commonalty; but how aptly, and how fitly, we offer unto you to determine.

Major

Major WILDMAN's Reply.

May it please your Lordship and this honourable Court to give me leave to make some Answers to what the learned Gentlemen on the other side have pleased to object and take exceptions at what was affirmed. I shall not (my Lord) endeavour (as that Gentleman did) *captare benevolentiam*, to take the affections of the people, before I begin to debate the matter in question. I shall not tell them that I will not insinuate into their mindes any thing but what will stand upon the foundation of truth; but offer my thoughts, and freely submit to your judgement. Yet I hope to answer particularly M *Maynard's* Exceptions.

He was pleased, first, to take exception at that general Principle that I averred, from whence I said might be deduced the Right of all the Wards to chuse the Lord Maior and Sheriffs by their Representatives: Though the Gentleman might have pleased to remember, I did say I would wave those Principles of common Right, left he should say we intended to bring all things to an uncertainty, by unravelling the bottom of Government to its first Principle; and therefore I insisted upon nothing but what we claim as our written Right. However, he might have pleased to spare quarrelling with that Principle, *That a just Subjection ought to be founded upon an assent of the People to their Governours power*; especially in this Parliamentary time, wherein the Parliament hath pleased to declare, *That the original of all just Power* (under God) *is from the People*. And how Governours shall derive a just power from the People, but by an Assent of the People, I understand not; neither do I know how we can otherwise be a Free People, as the Parliament hath declared we are. If he had quarrelled with this in the time of the King, it had been for his interest to have said, That we ought to be subject to the Son and Heir of a Conqueror, because such. I hope better things now.

The second thing the Gentleman was pleased to except against, was that which he onely imagined in his own brain, misreciting my words, like a man created by his fancy, to try his skill upon: for he supposed I did say, That if we had the Records that are now lost, we doubted not but that they would prove the assertion we maintain: whereas I said, *If we had the Records of those times, that are lost, they would shew us what the Rights of People then were*. And that I conceive to be without exception.

The next thing he takes exception against, is, what I said concerning *Magna Charta*; and would make this Court believe that I had thought all that great Charter was unalterable. I confess, if I had thought so, I would never have drawn Sword against the King. But the Gentleman
was

was pleafed to affert, That the King was by the Common Law ; and if he agrees with Sir *Edw. Cook's* Law, he faith that the Common Law is but *Recta Ratio*, Right Reafon ; and I am fure the King ftood not by Right Reafon: if he had, the Parlament could not have juftly declared his Office *burdenfome and unneceffary*. But the truth is, I did onely fay, That *Magna Charta*, the great Charter of *England*, was unalterable, according to the principles of the Gentlemen of the long Robe: I onely fpcke it upon their bottom. I faid, If I fhould believe Sir *Edw. Cook* in what he faid upon the Statute of 42 *Edw.* 3, I muft then fay, that an Act of Parliament made contrary to that part of the great Charter that was declarative of the Common Law, was null of it felf: for he faid that part of it was unalterable. Thus I give them onely their own authority, and made it no affertion of mine abfolutely: Though, under his favour, I think a man may affert, that what is founded upon the true Common Law of *England*, as Sir *Edw. Cook* faith, which is *Right Reafon*, no Authority whatfoever ought to alter: (I fpeak not of circumftances:) for if we fhould aver that, we fhould aver contradictions in the very terms, and fay, That *Right Reafon* of right may be altered from *Right Reafon.* I fhall let pafs what the Gentleman was pleafed to fay of the Laws being edge-tools, and of men cutting themfelves with them. I believe he met with an Argument for the Peoples Right that was an edge tool in his way; and he was loth to break his fhins over it, and therefore he paft over the Argument with a grave caution of the fharpnefs of the Law, that he might divert your thoughts from it. But the Gentleman coming a little nerer to the matter, lays down his Maxime, which is this, That ever fince the 15 of *Edward* the fourth, thefe Liveries have had the choice. And then he argues thus: Saith he, *The cafe would be very hard to have your titles of Land, after one hundred and ninety yeers poffeffion, to be queftioned: And is it not as hard, that the right of the Liveries to Elections fhould now be queftioned?* Under the Gentleman's favour, the cafe is very different. I fuppofe no man pleads for the like title to a Power or Authority over the People, that men have to their Lands, nor upon the fame grounds. If the Titles were alike, it were juft to buy and fell Authority, or Places of Truft and Government, as we buy and fell Lands, or Horfes in *Smithfield*; and this our Common Law abhors. If we fpeak of people that are arrant meer Vaffals, like the Slaves in *Argier*, Authority over them is indeed bought and fold; but I hope we are not to be fo efteemed; and yet the juftice of thofe bargains is not clear. But certainly mens Titles to Land, and to a power of Government, are, or ought to be of a different nature: And I fhall make bold to affert, That 'tis no hard Cafe, that the Right of any number of men claiming a power in or about Government by fucceffion onely, fhould after 190 yeers poffeffion be queftioned. Suppofe M. *Maynard* could have made good the Livery-mens claims to the election of the chief Officers of the City by cuftom, (but then he muft have more then

doubled

Major Wildmans Reply. 25

doubled the time of the usage he spake of,) yet I humbly conceive that the exercise of any Power about Government is not made just by continuance of time, unless it were just in the Original. If long Usurpation of a Power in or about Government could give a right to that Power, all the Foundations of just Government were overturned, and by Consequence it were not right or just to take away an usurped Power if the Usurpers be grown old.

Next, The Gentleman is pleased before he comes to his material Arguments, to insinuate strange, huge, dreadful, monstrous Consequences that would ensue, in case any man shall deny his Assertions, he is pleased to say, *what strange Consequences would ensue, if we should say, for 190 years all the Lord Majors or Sheriffs of the City of* London *have been unlawfully chosen?* Truly I could only answer, That we might have said, before the Parliament executed Justice upon the King and cast off his Family, what strange Consequences will ensue? If we should say, that almost for 500. years the people of *England* have been governed by them that came in unlawfully, and claimed their Power successively, to make the people their vassals, by the Sword of *William* the Conqueror, but the Parliament was not affrighted by such Bugbear Arguments to do Justice upon him, and take away the Power that his Family claimed by Conquest over us, and I believe Mr *Maynard* will not say they did unjustly. But suppose that which he suggests, that the Majors have been chosen unlawfully so long, 'tis time then to provide for a lawful Choyce; and the continuance of the unlawful will breed more of Mr *Maynards* monstrous Consequences; and if it be unlawful, 'tis not forbearing to say so that will amend the Consequences.

But now the Gentleman comes to his Position, and faith, *That this Government that is now is lawful.* The Gentleman might have pleased to have spared that; I did not yet assert that the Government that is now is unlawful; yet he may take some Answers to his Arguments, or rather Authorities for the legallity of it.

The first Ground he builds upon for the lawfulness of this Government is the Opinion of the Judges, which makes a huge Cry. But by the way, the Question is not now concerning the Government, but only concerning the Choosers or Electors of the Governors; the Government may be the same still, though the manner and way of electing these Governors may be altered from what it is at present. Yet to that Opinion of the Judges, which makes the great noise in the Court; *Oh* (faith he) *'tis the Opinion of all the learned Judges:* and then he paraphrases upon the goodness, honesty, learning and fame of the Judges that were named in the Book produced. It may be those Gentlemen of the Long-Robe were Black-Swans; yet the Argument from Authority is none of the strongest, 'Tis not a very good Consequence, that the thing is just because good men thought so.

D E   Yet

Yet under favour the Opinion of the Iudges I take to be not the most certain or unalterable amongst men, nor the most unbyassed by their own Interest. I beleeve if a man should go to the twelve Iudges, he shall scarce find four or three of the twelve of the same opinion in a dubious case; yet if there were more that agreed, the late Opinion of the Iudges in the case of Ship-mony may inform us how free the Iudges Opinions are from the Byas of private Interest in such cases, and how fit 'tis for us to depend upon them; They could many of them agree to destroy Property at once in favour of the King; but however the Opinion of the Iudges produced by Mr *Maynard*, I crave leave to affirm to be against him in this case, at least not for him. I desire it may be read.

The Case of Corporations, touching the Election of Governors in the fourth of the Lord Cooks Reports, fol. 77, 78.

In the same Term at Serjeants-Inn in Fleetstreet, it was demanded of the chief Iustices, *Popham*, and *Anderson*, and *Periam*, chief Baron, and of the other Iustices, That where divers Cities, Burroughs and Towns are incorporate by Charters, whether by the name of the Major & Commonalty, or the Major & Burgesses, and on the Bayliff and Burgesses, &c. or the Aldermen and Burgesses, or the Provost and Sheriffs, or Burgesses, or the like; and in the said Charters it be prescribed that the Major, Bayliffs, Aldermen, Provosts shall be chosen by the Commonalty or Burgesses, and of the ancient and usual Elections of Major, Bayliffs, Provosts, *and by a certain CHOSEN number of the chief of the Commonalty*, or of the Burgesses, commonly called the Common Councel, or by other name, and not in general by all the Commonalty or Burgesses, or not by so many of them as will come to the Election, shall be good in Law, forasmuch as by these words of the Charters the Election shall be *indefinitely* by the *Commonalty*, or all the Burgesses. And which Question being of great importance and consequence, was referred by the Lords of the Councel to the Iustices, to know the Law in that case; for that divers attempts were now of late in divers Corporations, contrary to the ancient usage, to make popular Elections; and it was resolved by the Iustices upon great deliberation, and upon Conference had amongst themselves, *that such ancient usual Elections* were good, and well warranted by their Charter, and by the Law also; for in every of their Charters they have power given them to make Laws, Ordinances, and Constitutions for the better Government and Order of their Cities or Burroughs, and by force of which, and for avoyding popular confusion, *they by their common assent constitute or ordain*, That the Major, Bayliffs, or other principal Officers, shall be chosen by *one certain Select number* of the principal of the Commonalty, or of the Burgesses, as is aforesaid

Major Wildmans Reply.

said, and prescribe also how *such Selected numbers* shall choose; and such Ordinances and Constitutions was resolved to be good, and allowable, and agreeable with the Law, and their Charters, for avoyding of popular Disorder and Confusion; and although that no such Constitution or Ordinance can be shewed, yet it shall be presumed and intended in respect of such special manner *of ancient and continual Election, which special Election is not begun without common Consent*; that at the first late Ordinance or Constitution was made, such reverend respect of Law doth give to *ancient and continual* allowance and usage, as it had been within time of memory. And the Custom of most faithful Antiquity is to be esteemed; The things which are done contrary to the custom and usage of the Ancients either please or seem right, and the frequence of the Act premiseth much, and according to that Resolution the ancient and continual Usages have been in the Cities of *London* and *Norwich*, and other ancient Cities and Corporations. And God defend that they shall be now innovated or altered, for that many and great inconveniencies will arise upon the same; all which the Law hath well prevented, as appears by that Resolution.

First, My Lord, observe, That the Question here resolved is not our Question, the Question here resolved was this, *whether an Election of a Major, not made by all the Commonalty in a Corporation, or at least as many as would come, was good in Law?* But our present Question is only this, *whether the Commonalty of this City ought not to have their Representers to choose the Lord Major?* So that we do grant, that an Election not made by all the Commonalty may be good.

Now, my Lord, observe the Judges Resolution of the Question; they resolve that an Election made by the Major and Aldermen, and a certain chosen number of the choyce of the Commonalty, is good in Law. We concur with the Judges, keeping close to their words, *A certain Chosen number of the Commonalty*; and to those other words of theirs, *viz. such ancient usual Elections*; that is to say, such ancient Elections by the chosen number of the Commonalty are good in Law. Now we deny that the present Election of the Lord Major by the Livery-men is the most ancient usual way of electing, and that the Livery-men are a chosen number of the Commonalty, I mean, chosen according to any right of choyce, that right being in the Commonalty.

But, my Lord, 'tis very observable in this Opinion of the Judges, upon what Ground they judged such Elections valid in Law; the Ground is this, *For 'tis to be imagined or supposed*, say they, *that such ancient and continued Elections did not begin without common assent.* Hence 'tis evident, that the Judges imagined that all the Citizens had the right of choyce in them, & that they had agreed that a chosen number of themselves should choose in their stead; So that the

D 2 Judges

Iudges in their Opinion took the chofen number of the chief of the Commonalty that did elect the chief Officers to be the Reprefenters of the whole Commonalty.

Now if your Lordfhip pleafe to remember we produced an Act of the Common Hall of *London*, made long before the Liveries made any claim to be the Choofers, and at an Affembly, when the Guild-Hall was filled with the Commonalty, wherein they did affent, that there fhould be a certain number of every Ward proportionably that fhould be the Electors of the Major and Sheriffs; So that the way we propofe, of feveral men of every Ward reprefenting the Wards to elect, is founded upon a common Affent. They produce no one Act of a common Hall, that fhould make it appear, that it was ever affented unto by the Commonalty, that the Livery men of the Myfteries fhould be the Choofers of the Major.

Now my Lord I humbly offer it to this honorable Court, Whether this opinion of the Judges about Elections, produced by Mr *Maynard* as the pillar whereon they build the lawfulnefs of the Liveries Elections, do not rather fpeak them to be unlawful, in my humble opinion, this that thofe learned gentlemen flourifhed like Goliah's fword againft us, flayes themfelves.

After Mr *Maynard* had produced the Authority of the Judges, as he fuppofed for his Clyents cafe, he argues from confequences, faith he, If this prefent way of Electing by the Liveries were not Lawful, marke the confequences, your Charter, faith he, is forfeited; this I confeffe is a big bellyd word, but how will this affertion agree with what Mr *Maynard*, Mr *Hales*, & Mr *wilde*, all affirmed, That the Charters of the City did not originally give the City thofe Liberties that are mentioned in the Charter, but that the Charters were only Declarative of the Cities rights, fhewing what their rights were before the Charters, now if the Charters give not the City their rights, certainly you cannot forfeit your Charters, unlefs the Learned Gentlemen fhall pleafe to fay, You fhall forfeit the Declaration of your rights (for the Charters are no more by their own confeffion) and if your forfeiture be no more you may enjoy your Liberties ftill, notwithftanding fuch a forfeiture as they pretend. But fuppofe a man fhould fay what I did not yet fay, That the prefent way of Electing the Mayor is unlawful, is it any more then this, that the Citizens have fuffered their right to be taken from them for many years, and others to enjoy it unlawfully, and how will this confequence be deduced from thence, That the City hath forfeited their rights; I confeffe I underftand not by the Law that a body Politique or Corporation, as fuch, is under harder Laws in our Nation then the Members of the Common-wealth feverally; now no man in England can forfeit his rights without a Legal conviction of fome crime for which the Law cenfures him to forfeit his rights; and I know no reafon why

the

Major Wildmans Reply.

the City should have such hard measure, that in case the free men have suffered the Companies to usurp their right, that therefore all the Cities rights should be forfeited. But without question this Argument might have frighted you in the Kings time, then some needy projecting Courtier might have frighted you with the forfeiture of your Charter to the King, and eased you of some of your bags, upon pretence of soliciting the King to renew your Charter for an easie Fine; but now if you be satisfied you have erred from the Rule. I beleeve you may return to do right and enjoy your Liberties without paying a fine.

Mr *Maynards* next Argument for the Liveries Elections was this, That tis founded upon a constant usage time out of mind, so that, saith he, the City now prescribes unto this way of Electing; and yet the Gentleman was pleased afterwards to confesse, that to make a title by prescription there must be a constant usage since *Rich.* the first time, and they only produce an Act of a Common Councel for the Liveries Electing about 174 years since, and will suppose that that Act of Common Councel was in confirmation of what was the custom before, whereas they produce no one footstep of a Record before that time to prove that it was the usage to chuse by Livery-men, but on the contrary it hath appeared that the Election hath been 400 years since by a select number out of the several Wards, which cannot be any way supposed to be meant of Livery-men, they not coming as men from several Wards, but as men from several Companies.

The next thing the Gentleman said, was this, That he hoped we would grant that we did both depart from the Charter it self; for, saith he, if we found the way of electing upon the Charter, the Charter running to the Citizens indefinitely, it must be understood of all the Citizens and Barons; and, saith he, you grant, it is impossible they should all together make the Election, so we both depart from it. Under his favor I must be bold to deny it; We depart not from the Charter, for we say, that the Charter giving a right of choyce to all the Citizens, they may proceed in their Elections, either by themselves personally, or their Deputies; and they finding it inconvenient to meet personally, may depute others to make their Elections; and an Election so made is truly said to be made by the Citizens. So that in case that way of Electing were admitted which the Petitioners propose, it were directly agreeable to the Charter; for then indeed the Citizens should chuse, because they chuse every one of them by their Deputies, as all the People of England make Laws in Parliament, because every mans Deputy is, or ought to be, there in Parliament.

Next Mr *Maynard* answers an Objection; If, saith he, it be objected, that in the way of Election that is by the Livery-men, all are not represented; saith he, it is true, if you take it in some sence; but

but, saith he, if you take it in the sence of the Law, therein they are represented, and it is the City makes these Elections; Saith he, the Law faith so; as, faith he, in cafe a mans hand moves, it is the man that moves, or his eye fees a colour, it is the man that fees. I hope the Gentleman will please to confess a vast difference between a Body natural, and a Body politique; Becaufe he may truly fay, if a mans hand moves, all the man moves, therefore will he fay that what a few, or one member of the City doth, is the Cities action? If so, if one in the City commit Treason, all the City are Traytors. I beleeve, Gentlemen, you would be loath to admit of such a Law.

But to confirm this affertion the Gentleman produced fomething out of that which he called *Articuli fuper Chartas*, where he faith, the King granted to the People to chufe Sheriffs, and yet the people did not chufe them all in general, it was the Freeholders chofe them. Mr *Maynard*, if he pleafeth, co ld have told when the People in general were reftrained from electing Parliament-men, and other the Sheriffs alfo, and upon what pretence it was put upon Freeholders onely, and how it ferved the Kings ends to procure that Statute of Reftriction; if I forget not the time, it was in the 8 of *Henry 6*. Chap. 7. But however Mr *Maynard* fhould have proved this to be juft, before he can prove the other to be juft by this.

Now the Gentleman is pleafed to come to examine the prefidents we produced, and faith, he will turn our own fwords into our own bowels; and endevors to do it thus;

Firft, faith he, you prove that the Wards did fend feveral perfons to thefe Elections 400 years fince, but you prove not that the Wards chofe thefe perfons; you read indeed Records that faid thefe perfons were fummoned to the Election, but who fummoned them? certainly the Major fummoned them, and he fummoned whom he would. I verily beleeve this would be a very bitter pill for the Citizens to digeft, to fay the Lord Major fhould fummon when he pleafed, and whom he pleafed, out of every Ward to come to the Election, the Government would be turned topfie turvy, if that were admitted, then he that fhould be once Lord Major, might be for ever Lord Major, if he could make but a friend or two in every Ward, and if this be imagined to have been the cuftom of the City, I wonder who fummoned thofe that chofe the firft Major.

But the Gentleman is pleafed to make his Argument thus; faith he, it is not named in the Record you produce, that thefe men were elected by the Wards, though fummoned from the Wards, therefore faith he, they were not elected. It is a new kinde of Logick that

muft

Major VVildmans Reply. 31

must make this Argument good; *'Tis not recited in the Record that they were chosen, therefore they were not chosen*; I might as well say that in your summon to a Common Councel, your being chosen by the Wards is not recited, therefore you Gentlemen of this Court were not chosen. I confess I am not very well verst in the Acts that are in this Court, but I think there is no Act of the Court recorded, wherein it is said, *there were present the Common Councel that were chosen by such Wards*, shall I therefore conclude that they were not chosen by the Wards? I must first learn a new Logick, before I shall dare so to conclude.

The second thing he objected against the presidents, was this, Those twelve men of the Wards that are said to elect the Major, saith he, must needs be understood to be Common councel men; Truly, besides the Answer of Mr *Price*, that it was not probable, because the number of Common-councel would then have been far greater, then now it is, when the City was far less; to let that pass, I onely answer thus, that if they please to look in 22 of *Henry* the sixth, it is in Lib. K. fol. 214. it is said in the Writ that came down from the King to prevent disturbances at that Election of the Major, that none should be there but they that had an interest to be there, those that were in Common-councel, *and the more discreet and able men of the wards*, so that besides the common councel, there were others that were wise and able discreet men in the Wards that were to come to the Elections, which probably were those that were chosen by the Wards. If your Honor please the Record may be read. The former Answer serves to Mr *Maynards* Observation of the Election of the Parliament men for the city, wherein it is said only six of a Ward were called to be there, but not chosen; I propose it to him, whether it is probable that the Lord Major had power to pick six men out of a ward to chuse the Parliament men for the city, or whether this be a good Argument, because they are said to be summoned by the Lord Major, and not said to be elected, therefore they were not elected. I hope the Gentlemen of the long Robe have better Arguments.

The last thing that Mr *Maynard* avers, is, the inconveniencies in point of Law that would ensue upon that which we pray for, which he calls an Innovation. But I humbly crave leave to aver, unless I could see his confutation, that it is an ancient Right of the Citizens of this City. Those inconveniences in point of Law, he saith, are these, the hazard of forfeiting of *Charters*. I conceive that to be answered before, That if a city should depart from a just way, if their *Charter* were but the confirmation of their Right before, there is no forfeiting of that *Charter*, for the *Charter* gives them not that Right.

The

The next Argument he draws from every mans living in a *Court Lett*, and that at twelve years old he ought to meet there, and he faith from thence, if there should be Reprefenters of the Wards chofen, to make the choyce, it might be that thofe that are no citizens might meet to chufe a Major, and citizens that live without fhould not chufe. I think under his favor the common practice will anfwer to that, when the Wards meet for the choyce of Aldermen, or common councel men, none but citizens have their Votes in it, there is no danger that thofe that are aliens fhould either be chofen or choofers.

His next Argument againft this Petition is this, faith Mr *Maynard*, *It will tend to Popularity, if this should be admitted, that the wards should choofe; and I leave it,* faith he, *to the Court to judg what the Confequent of that would be; all mens Educations,* faith he, *are not fuch as make them fit for Government, or fit to choofe Governors.* Truly if it pleafe the honorable court but to confider who they are that are now the Electors, this Arrow of the Gentlemans returns upon himfelf I could fay more of it, if I fhould not be thought to reflect, becaufe I have a reverend refpect to all kind of Trades; but if I fhould fpeak of all the feveral Companies, the Bricklayers, Bowyers, Fletchers, Turners, Coopers, Tallow-Chandlers, &c. if I fhould fpeak of the Education of moft of the Livery men of forty Companies of the City, and compute their number, and tell you upon what terms moft are admitted to be of the Liveries, that is, for a fmall fum of money; I conceive the Court would quickly judg which way of Election tends moft to Popularity, as he calls it, and who propofeth moft men that are unfit for Government, to choofe the Lord Major and Sheriffs. Will any man fuppofe that the Educations of all the Handicraft men of the Liveries render them fo able and difcreet, that they are fit for Government? I fubmit it to the Court.

As for the great Word Mr *Maynard* was pleafed to add about the ill confequents of this change that would be to other Corporations, faying, *That this is as Earthquake comes under them.* I fhall conceive his Oratory in this to be of the Earthquakes nature, a fwelling vapor, unlefs he will be pleafed to fhew me how the Liberty of the City, or any one Citizen, is undermined by what is propofed; only I muft obferve to the Court, that where Arguments are wanting, their room is commonly fupplyed with words and pretences of huge ftrange confequences, that will infue, if their defires be croffed; But the Arguments from a confequence, I believe they well know their ftrength is not of the firft degree; but however to fuppofe an ill confequence my enfue upon a *City*, or compauy of perfons exercifing their right, and thence to conclude they muft not enjoy it, is a way of arguing that I underftand not.

I confess M. Ha'es is pleased to deal very ingenuously in laying down those principles wherein we agreed, which was, That the Liberties of the City were by prescription, and that the Charters were but Declarations of what our Liberties were, and that the Common-Councel-men ought to have a Vote in their Elections; But I said not they ought, but that they might have their Votes if they were chosen to that purpose: But he was pleased to say, that the Lord Maior, Aldermen, and Common-Counsel, were a kind of a Representative of the City, and therefore he would thence aver, that there is no inconvenience to the City, seeing they have such a Representative. I shall answer M. Hales thus, If a man should say the Parliament represent the Common-wealth, and seing we have a Representative, what matter if that 200. or 300. men more went into the Parliament and voted with them, the people of *England* surely would not think themselves well dealt withall, nor think those Acts so passed to be valid. M. Hales is pleased also to pursue M. Maynards mode of imagining strange kind of consequences that may ensue upon this, and saith he, How if the people will say, when you brought it to the Representatives, we will not be bound to Representatives, but we will come and chuse personally; what then (saith he) would be the consequence of this? Truly if M. Hales will suppose that the people will not be bound by any Government, not by Acts of Parliament, he may fill his fancy with bad consequences: and why may it not be supposed as well, that all the people in *England* should say, we will go and make Laws our selves in Parliament, as well as that the people should not be willing to be bound in their Wards to chuse the Lord Maior and Sheriffs by their Representatives? I shall let pass also what M. Hales was pleased to urge concerning that principle of a just subjection of people to Governours, to be founded upon an Assent, because he was pleased to confess very ingenuously, that I waved those Arguments that might reduce Government to an uncertainty, or to the first principles of general Common Right. But saith M. Hales, if that principle be allowed amongst a free people, that subjection to their Governours ought to be by meer assent,; saith he. we must consider there is a Personal and a Virtual assent, and it shall be conceived to be a Virtual consent, where there hath been an usage time out of mind for the People to be subject to any form of Government. Of which nature he endeavoured to prove the way of electing the Lord Maior and Sheriffs by the Livery-men of the several Mysteries; whereas if M Hales please to remember, they do all aver the usage of this way of Electing, but to have been for 174. yeers that they can prove. As for any suppositions that it was before, I think there is enough answered to that, there being no ancienter Records that mention the choise to have been by the Livery men, who come not as sent from Wards. And though M. Hales is pleased to ballance the Records produced on one hand and on the other, and saith thus, that they produce for one hundred seventy four yeers, to shew

E. F that

that this hath been the way of electing which now is; but faith he, those Records produced to prove another way of electing, is but a short time. If he please to remember there is no foot-step or mention made of any Livery-men, or of any of the Mysteries having a Vote to elect, until that 15. of *Edw.* 4. and we find from *Edward* the first, about 200 years before, that there were twelve men in the Wards that were Electors, which we may well think to be the Representors of those Wards, and chosen by them for that purpose; and no foot-steps of the discontinuance of it, from that time produced; but we may well say that all the Records that mention the Communalties choice, are to be interpreted by the former Records, until that Record comes wherein mention is made of Livery-men, there being no mention made of them formerly, under that, or any other name as such.

That which he was pleased to alledge, that it was the Common-Council-men that were those twelve men, is answered before in M. *Maynards*, and therefore I pass it over.

But M. *Hales* seem to think it hard measure that we should exclude the Livery because there is no mention made of them. I shall onely answer, that it is as hard for them to say, because the Common Counsel men are not mentioned to joyn with the 12 of the Wards, therefore they were excluded. But faith M. *Hales*, it is the Usage that shall explain what is meant by the Communalty, and what is meant by those more able and discreet men in the City that are chosen; we desire but to stand to the explanation of the Record; we produced an ancient Record that had these words, viz. *The whole Communalty;* that is to say, the more able and discreet men of the Ward; we would fain have him produce a Record where it is said, The whole Communalty, that is to say, the Livery men, at least any time before that of *Edward* the fourth.

As to the Arguments from the consequences, if this Government were not right, then faith M. *Hales*, all the purchases you have made since that time you altered the way of Elections, is null.

I must humbly crave leave not to submit to his judgement in that, till he give me better reasons; for I suppose it is grounded upon that of forfeiting a Charter, which was answered before; for though the Body corporate have not had their Officers rightly elected, yet the Body is not thereby dissolved, and therefore their purchase may be good, and without fear of forfeiture.

The Arguments M. *Wild* was pleased to use, were but to inforce what his brethren had said, that the 12 Electors of the Wards must be meant the Common-Council, because (faith he) no mention is made of the Common-Council; but it hath bin proved that in an election mention is made of the Common-Council, and of other honest men of the City, before any mention is made of Livery men; and though no mention were made of the Common Council, yet to say they were not

mentioned

Major Wildmans *Reply.*

mentioned, therefore they were not called to that Assembly when this Election was made, is no good consequence; upon the grounds before asserted, M. *Wilds* objection that we would endeavour to introduce a novelty, falls to the ground; for we conceive the way of 12. men out of the Wards to be far more ancient than the way that is now practised. And as for M. *Wilds* Arguments concerning the danger that would ensue upon the multitude coming to Elections, upon the same ground he may say, the Wards must not chuse their Aldermen nor Common Councel men, if the Citizens should be deprived of their right, upon that ground, that it is popularity, or they may be divided, and fall to blows; upon the same grounds they may take away the liberty of chusing Common Councel men, and Aldermen, and all their common Freedoms; and if these fears shall affright men from the claim of their Right, they may be told next that the Sky may fall, and therefore they must not go abroad.

As for the last objection of M. *Wilds*, that in this way of popularity 'tis possible a choise may be made of unfit men. I shall onely offer this to the consideration of the Court, Whether it is more probable that a whole Ward meeting together to chuse a small number of men that should represent them in the electing their Superiour Officers, should chuse more unfit men for that Election, then a company it may be of Coopers, Tallow-chandlers, or other manual occupations should admit to the Livery, who admit all that will give so much money to be of the Livery; who are the likelyest men to send fittest men for the choice, I humbly refer to the Honourable Court, though it is strange to me to hear that the fear of popularity, or of giving way so much to the Liberty of the people, is so much insisted on, now we are come into the way of a Common-Wealth; it is a little dissonant to the present constitution.

Now I shall humbly submit to the Court what hath been offered in answer to that which the Gentlemen on the other side have objected; and humbly crave leave to be still of opinion, that I see nothing of strength objected against our Assertion, *viz.* That the liberty of Electing is the Right of the Citizens of *London* in general, and so declared by the first Charter we find upon Record; And if it be the liberty of the Citizens in general to chuse, every man must chuse either by himself or deputy; and they all agree it is impossible they should all chuse personally, why they should not then chuse by their Representatives, I humbly leave to the judgement of this Honourable Court.

M. Maynard.

WE have taken up a great deal of time and patience, I will repeat nothing of what hath been said, only I think M. *Wildman* fears nothing of a popularity ; for the matter, the measure is before you, how long one, how long another, we differ upon the Records recited, we think they are for us, they think the contrary ; it lies in your judgements, and the measure of time how much it is ; I am sure they cited no Presidents before *Edward* the first's time, and none since *Edward* the third's time ; somwhat was spoken of *Henry* the sixt ; I will not enter into a particular recapitulation, but there hath been nothing of that I apprehend we have said, but hath been answered onely by the by ; and that which is the strength of that we rely upon, hath been let go, and some generals taken hold of only ; I shall give you but this observation, that it is like enough the Maior and Sheriffs, the Chamberlain who is the keeper of all the wealth of the City, and the great trust of the City reposed in them, will much depend upon this string ; Two Gentlemen have here argued, and observe it, the one grants what the other will not, we all agree, and how they will agree when a great many come together, I leave it to you to judge.

M. Hales.

Onely this, Gentlemen, some two or three little mistakes there have been : I think not that they are wilful.

First of all, Whereas they would offer it to you, that the words *of all the Commonalty*, should be intended of the twelve men of the Wards, that is mistaken : for, Gentlemen, it was in a case of a choice of Aldermen, which is made by the Wards, and is not made by twelve men, as the very Record it self speaks ; and therefore that is misapplied. It is in case of a choice of Aldermen, which is made by the Wards in their bulks ; and not in twelve men.

And then next of all, for the continual Usage, they mistake in that. For that Usage, they give an instance in the third of King *Edward* the first, till some later time in *Edward* the second, and in the twentieth of *Edward* the third : But from the twentieth of *Edw*. the third, not any instance at all of electing men out of Wards. That which they say now they are driven to it, now they would indeed exclude the Common Councel from having any voice of right. We say, You do well. If the Common Councel have no right, then may the Livery-men have no right neither ; for their Rights will stand and fall upon the same bottom. We say onely this : For that Record of *Henry* the sixth's time, it's nothing at all to the purpose ; for that is this, That all those that were in the Common Councel, together with other persons that were
called

called in, either from the Wards or City, be it which it will: there is no man doubts but most of the Liveries they live in the Wards; and therefore it is not an argument that they were not persons that were of the Wards. And whereas we have no footsteps of the Livery in Record, it is true, the stiling of the Record is not of the Liveries; your Elections are not said to be by the Liveries at this day, but by the Commonalty, as it was neer two hundred yeers ago; and yet in truth done by the Common Councel and Lveries: so that all is one.

M. *Wild.*

My Lord, I shall onely desire M. *Latham* may read this Record in the twentieth of *Edw.* the third; it is that whereupon I built my Argument; that is, Thus it was agreed by all the commonalty of the City, that the Lord Maior for the time being shall be chosen by twelve, eight, or six out of every Ward, according to the greatness or bigness of the Ward. That must of necessity be the Common Councel.

M. *Maynard.*

One thing I forgot in that, That your Livery-men come not by number; Common Councel-men they are summoned by a certain number.

¶ *Here the Record was read.*

M. *Hales.*

This is that we say, and here we leave it. We say, That that Reason that these Gentlemen do use upon their presidents in *Edward* the first's time, and *Edward* the second's time, is to exclude the Common Councel, as well as the common Hall; and we say, that upon the same reasons they may exclude the one as well as the other. There is no mention made of the common-Councel to have a voice in any of the Elections in Records, and therefore they would exclude them. We say, They do the Record and themselves wrong; for though it's truth, there is mention made of the Maior, Aldermen, and some others, it is not exclusive; for some others there might be, and yet notwithstanding it is agreed that the Common-councel may make an election, and vote, and are not excluded; and therefore the Livery-men may do the same. And wheñs it hath gone on so long, and not been contradicted, we hope you will continue on that continued course.

M. *Wildman.*

My Lord, We still insist upon it, that those presidents produced, being for twelve men out of every Ward, cannot probably be conceived to be the Common-councel; for how can we conceive that the Common councel, at that time when the city was not a fourth part of what it is, should consist of as many or more then it doth now? But by the Record now read, it appears, that it was agreed that so many men of every Ward should come to the election; and then further agreed, that every Alderman of every Ward should cause such a number, a smaller number then the other, to be chosen, to be of the Common councel; and
'tis

'tis not said that they should be the electors. The Record speaks of two things agreed unto: First, that one number of men should be elected for the Wards; secondly, that another number of men should be chosen by the Wards, to consult, as the Record saith, *de arduis negotiis*, to consult about the hard matters that concerned the city.

But suppose I should grant the learned Gentlemen of the other side that which they so much contend for, *viz.* That the twelve men of the Wards, mentioned in the Records to be the electors of the Maior, were the common councel; and that, as M. *Wild* would have it, the twelve, eight, or six of every Ward, that the common Hall agreed in the 20 of *Edw.* 3. should be the chusers of the Maior, that those were the common councel; suppose this, What advantage to their cause will the Gentlemen gain from thence? The conclusion from thence would be, That the common councel were the onely electors of the Maior; and what becomes of the Companies Liveries, for whose power in electing they plead? And if it were the common councel that were the electors, it doth establish our foundation, which is this, That all those who are chosen by the Wards, and do represent them, ought to chuse the chief Officers of the city. And if the Wards would trust the common councel onely to be the chusers now, and declare it in the choice of them, we should not oppose it.

M. *Maynard.*

Gentlemen, I forgot one word that M. *Wildman* was pleased to deliver for Law, that you may believe, if you think good, *That there is no forfeiture of Charters.* Now what the Parliment may do under favour, is no question; but no doubt but there is forfeiture of *Charters*. And he saith, *Twelve Judges there are, and but few of them agree.* You must be sure, That it is the Judges part to judge your actions at last.

FINIS.